De.

Adding

Ann Montague-Smith

QEB Publishing

Published in the United States by
QEB Publishing, Inc.
23062 La Cadena Drive
Laguna Hills, CA 92653

www.qeb-publishing.com

Library of Congress Control Number: 2005921183

ISBN 1-59566-096-8

Written by Ann Montague–Smith
Designed and edited by The Complete Works
Illustrated by Peter Lawson
Photography by Steve Lumb

Publisher Steve Evans
Creative Director Louise Morley
Editorial Manager Jean Coppendale

779 4969

Printed and bound in China

With thanks to:

Contents

Counting on

Look at each of the 2 sets of cats. Find the larger set and count how many. Keep that number in your head and count on for the smaller set. What number do you get to?

set 1

set 2

set 1

set 2

Which sets total 9?

set 1

set 2

Challenge

You will need 9 counters.
How many different ways can
you make 2 sets that total 9?
Write addition sentences
using + and = to show your sets.

$1 + 8 = 9$

set 1

set 2

set 1

set 2

5

Adding small numbers

Which 2 sets add up to 8? Find out by counting on in ones from the larger number. How many different ways can you do this?

Which 3 sets add up to 12?
Find 3 different ways to do this.

6

Now try this

Add 4 sets together.
What different totals can you make?
Write them as addition sentences.
Use + and = like this.

$$1+2+3+4=10$$

7

Totals of 10

Find 2 sets that add up to 10.

How many different ways can you do this?

Now try this

You will need 10 counters and a friend.
Take some of the counters.
Don't tell your friend how many you have.
Now ask your friend to count how many are
left. Can he/she say how many you took?
Now switch roles.

9

Adding to 10

Play this game with a friend. You will need some counters in two colors. Take turns to choose a number from both circle 1 and circle 2. Add the numbers together. Cover your answer on the bears' picnic blanket with a counter. The winner is the one with the most counters on the blanket.

circle 1

1 **2**
3 **4**

circle 2

1 **2**
6 **3**
5 **4**

10
2
3
1
1
6
2
3

Play again, but this time choose 2 numbers each time from the picnic blanket which you think total 10. Cover both numbers with counters if you are correct.

Challenge

Use a 1–6 dice.
Throw the dice twice.
Write an addition sentence
with the two numbers using
+ and =. Do this 4 times.

6+3=9

6

5

8

7

5

7

8

3

9

4

9

4

11

Doubles and near doubles

Play this game with a friend. You will need a 1–6 dice and two counters. Take turns to throw the dice. Move that number on the board. Add the numbers you land on. If you get it wrong, move your counter back to where you were before. The winner is the first one to the finish.

2+1

1+1

1+1

5+5

4+4

2+2

3+3

Try these strategies. For doubles, count on in ones like this, 4 and 5, 6, 7, 8. For near doubles, double and add 1 like this, 4+4+1.

1+2

3+2

6+6

4+3

2+3

3+4

5+4

6+5

4+5

5+6

Now try this

Use the numbers 6, 7, 8, 9, and 10. Double them. Now can you find near doubles such as 6+7, 7+8, and 8+9? Write some addition sentences for your doubles and near doubles.

6+6=
7+8=

13

Using 5

You will need some counters and a coin. Throw the coin onto the spinner. Split the spinner number into 5 and what's left over. So 9 would be 5+4. Now add 5 to 5+4. Cover your answer on one of the stars with a counter.

spinner

6 7
8 9

11

13

12

Throw the coin 5 more times.
Can you do these additions really quickly now?

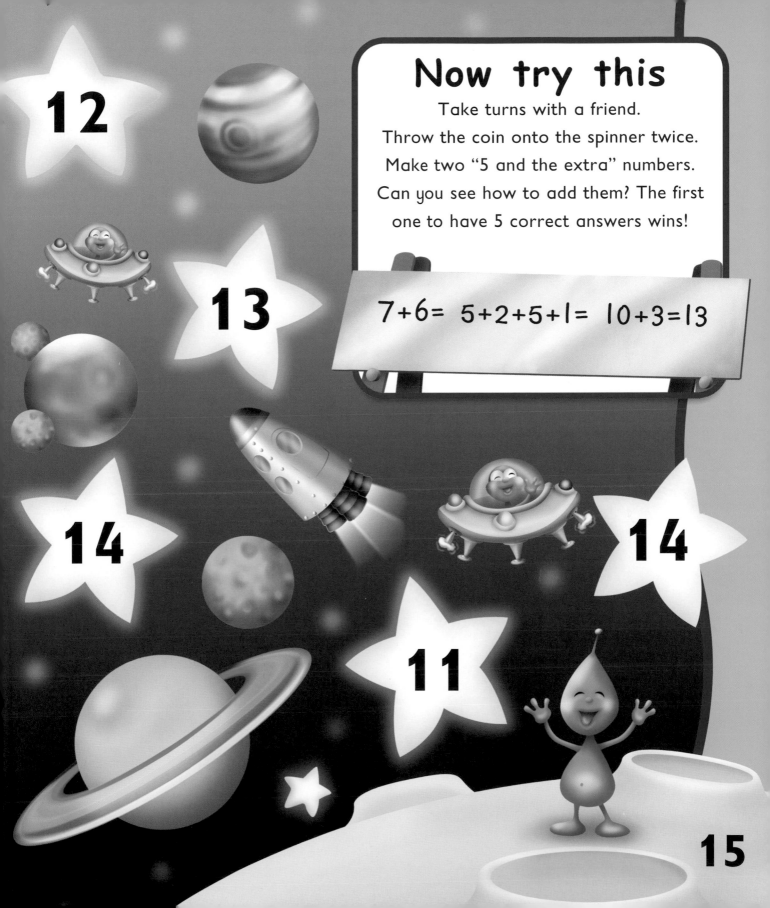

12

13

14

14

11

15

Now try this

Take turns with a friend.
Throw the coin onto the spinner twice.
Make two "5 and the extra" numbers.
Can you see how to add them? The first
one to have 5 correct answers wins!

7+6=   5+2+5+1=   10+3=13

Adding 9 and 11

There is a trick you can use when adding 9. For example, take 6+9. Think of 6+10. Now take away 1. These dogs have some bones. They have hidden 9 more. How many bones has each dog in total?

Suppose the dogs had hidden 11 bones. Try +10 then +1. How many bones has each dog now?

Challenge

The dogs have hidden 8 bones this time. Think about how you could work this out by adding 10. What would you need to take away?

Where have I buried my bones?

17

Adding 'teen numbers

Look at the numbers on each square. Find the total of each pair. Remember, if you know that 5+4=9 then you can see that 15+4=19.

Add 1 to each square. What is the total of each pair now?

Challenge

Write down these addition sentences.
10+4= 11+4= 12+4= Can you find
the answers? What would the next
sentence be? And the next one?
Tell an adult about the patterns
you can see.

An addition problem

Here are some boxes of toys. Each box shows you how many toys are inside. Imagine that you want 15 toys. Which boxes would you choose?

8

3

1

10

14

5

How many different ways can you choose 15 toys?

Challenge

Find different ways to choose 20 toys. Write an addition sentence each time.

11+9=20

4

12

6

11

9

7

13

2

21

Supporting notes

Counting on, pages 4–5

Putting the larger set first and counting on for the second set is a very useful mental strategy. Ask the children to count on in ones. They may find it helpful to keep a check by using their fingers so that they count on for the correct amount. For example, 6+3 is 6 and 7, 8, 9. The children put up three fingers, one at a time, to check their counting.

Adding small numbers, pages 6–7

Encourage the children to count on in ones from the larger number. For example, for 5+6 say 6 and 7, 8, 9, 10, 11. So 5+6 is 11. The children can keep track of the mental count using their fingers. Encourage the children to write an addition sentence using + and =.

Totals of 10, pages 8–9

The children find it helpful to use their fingers at first. Say, "I'll say a number. You show me with your fingers how many more I will need to make 10." The children can then use their 10 fingers to find the answer.

Adding to 10, pages 10–11

The children need to have rapid recall of all addition to at least 5+5, and then begin to know all addition to 10+10. Encourage them to use strategies such as "Put the larger number in your head and then count on from it in ones," when they do not have rapid recall of adding up to 10.

Doubles and near doubles, pages 12–13

The children find the strategy of counting on from one of the numbers helpful.
Where it is a near double, suggest that they count on from the smaller number and add 1.
Some children may prefer to count on from the larger number and subtract 1.
This is also a good strategy.

Using 5, pages 14–15

Discuss the strategy of breaking down a number using 5. Take 5+8. This is the same as
5+5+3 or 10+3. If the children are beginning to understand about place value, then they
will not need to add the 3 to the 10, instead they will see that 10+3=13, because
the "3" moves directly to the ones place.

Adding 9 and 11, pages 16–17

Understanding place value will help the children to see that if 10 is added to any number, then
it leaves the ones place unchanged. For example, 6+10 is 16. If the children are unsure, use a number
line so they can count on 10, then add/subtract 1 to complete the calculation.

Adding 'teen numbers, pages 18–19

Encourage the children to use what they already know, or can calculate mentally, in
order to figure out what they don't know. If the children are unclear about moving from,
for example, 5+3=8 to 15+3=18, then use a number line and show them how this is
the same as 10+5+3.

An addition problem, pages 20–21

The children may find it helpful to write out the numbers on the boxes onto some squares
of paper. Then ask them to try different combinations of their "boxes" to find totals of 15.
Some children may find a number line from 0 to 20 useful as an aid to calculating. They can
count along the line. However, encourage mental counting to find the totals.

Using this book

The illustrations in this book are bright, cheerful, and colorful, and are designed to capture children's interest. Sit somewhere comfortable together as you look at the book. Children of this age will usually need to have the instructional words on the pages read to them. Please read these out to them, then encourage them to take part in the activity.

In this book, children are encouraged to work both practically, by counting pictures on the pages, and by working mentally, such as counting "in their heads." The range of totals for adding extends from up to 10, then up to 20. Children are encouraged to use strategies of counting on from the larger number in ones; finding two 5s to make a 10 and adding on, such as 5+6=5+5+1=10+1; and extending this to adding on 10 and adjusting by 1, such as in 9+5=10+5-1; learning double facts to 5+5, then deriving near doubles from this such as 4+5=4+4+1 or 5+5-1. For strategies that involve adding beyond 10, children will need to learn about place value; for example, that for any 'teen number, such as 13; the 1 stands for "10" and the 3 for "3 ones."

For some children, counting along a number line can help. Either draw a 0–10 or 0–20 number line, or use a simple ruler or yardstick. Then children can use the tool to add up.

Some of the activities in this book are games for two or more to play together. Play the game, too, and make some "deliberate" mistakes. This will challenge the children to see the mistake and correct you. This will also help you assess how well the children understand and can use the mathematical idea on the page.

Learning about mathematics should always be a positive experience. So, enjoy the mathematical games, activities, and challenges in this book together!